SOUTH KOREA

...in Pictures

Visual Geography Series®

SOUTH KOREA

...in Pictures

Prepared by
Geography Department

Lerner Publications Company
Minneapolis

Photo by David Tykol

Some South Koreans still practice the ancient Chinese art of calligraphy (ornate handwriting).

This is an all-new edition of the Visual Geography Series. Previous editions have been published by Sterling Publishing Company, New York City, and some of the original textual information has been retained. New photographs, maps, charts, captions, and updated information have been added. The text has been entirely reset in 10/12 Century Textbook.

LIBRARY OF CONGRESS CATALOGING-IN-PUBLICATION DATA

> **South Korea in pictures.**
>
> (Visual geography series)
> Rev. ed. of: Korea, North & South, in pictures / prepared by William H. Mathews.
> Includes index.
> Summary: Describes the geography, history, government, people, and economy of South Korea.
> 1. Korea (South) [1. Korea (South)] I. Mathews, William H. Korea, North & South, in pictures. II. Lerner Publications Company. Geography Dept. III. Series: Visual geography series (Minneapolis, Minn.)
> DS902.S684 1989   951.9'5   89-2283
> ISBN 0-8225-1868-6

International Standard Book Number: 0-8225-1868-6
Library of Congress Catalog Card Number: 89-2283

VISUAL GEOGRAPHY SERIES®

Publisher
Harry Jonas Lerner
Associate Publisher
Nancy M. Campbell
Senior Editor
Mary M. Rodgers
Editors
Gretchen Bratvold
Dan Filbin
Photo Researcher
Karen A. Sirvaitis
Editorial/Photo Assistant
Marybeth Campbell
Consultants/Contributors
Cheol Bae Son
Sandra K. Davis
Designer
Jim Simondet
Cartographer
Carol F. Barrett
Indexers
Kristine S. Schubert
Sylvia Timian
Production Manager
Gary J. Hansen

Photo by David Tykol

Both traditional and Western-style architecture stands on the grounds of the capitol building in Seoul.

Acknowledgments

Title page photo courtesy of Korean Overseas Information Services.

Elevation contours adapted from *The Times Atlas of the World*, seventh comprehensive edition (New York: Times Books, 1985).

1 2 3 4 5 6 7 8 9 10 99 98 97 96 95 94 93 92 91 90 89

Photo by R. K. Hur

University students, who are a politically active segment of South Korean society, march at a rally held in August 1988.

Contents

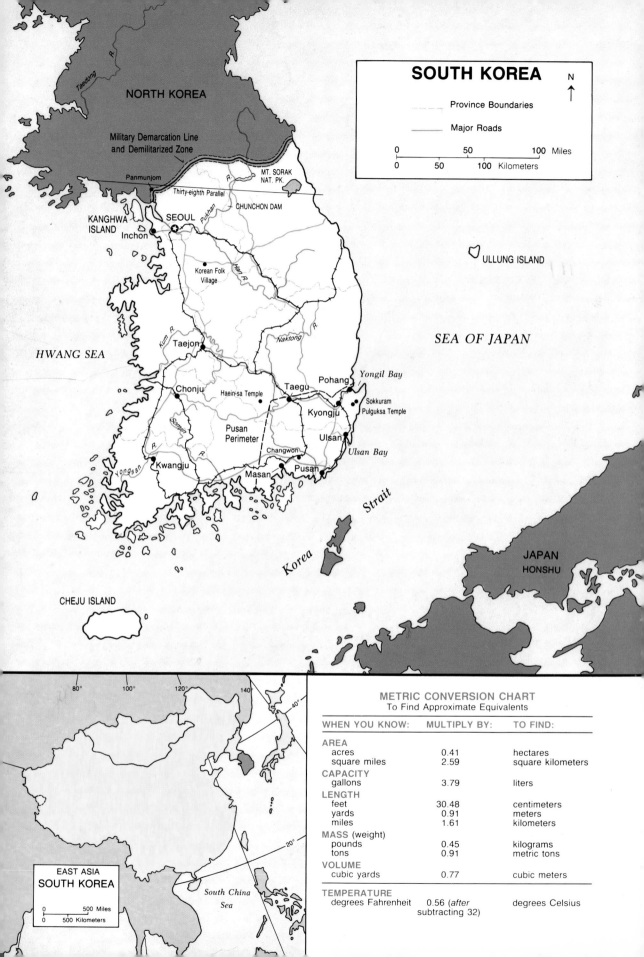

SOUTH KOREA

N

Province Boundaries

Major Roads

0   50   100 Miles
0   50   100 Kilometers

NORTH KOREA

Taedong R.

Military Demarcation Line
and Demilitarized Zone

Panmunjom

Thirty-eighth Parallel

MT. SORAK
NAT. PK.

CHUNCHON DAM

KANGHWA
ISLAND

Inchon

SEOUL

Pukhan R.

Han R.

Korean Folk
Village

ULLUNG ISLAND

Kum R.

Taejon

Naktong R.

HWANG SEA

Chonju

Haein-sa Temple

Taegu

Pohang

Yongil Bay

SEA OF JAPAN

Kyongju

Sokkuram
Pulguksa Temple

Somun R.

Pusan
Perimeter

Ulsan

Ulsan Bay

Yongsan R.

Kwangju

Changwon

Masan

Pusan

Korea Strait

JAPAN
HONSHU

CHEJU ISLAND

80°   100°   120°   140°

40°

20°

EAST ASIA
SOUTH KOREA

0   500 Miles
0   500 Kilometers

*South China
Sea*

METRIC CONVERSION CHART
To Find Approximate Equivalents

WHEN YOU KNOW:	MULTIPLY BY:	TO FIND:
AREA		
acres	0.41	hectares
square miles	2.59	square kilometers
CAPACITY		
gallons	3.79	liters
LENGTH		
feet	30.48	centimeters
yards	0.91	meters
miles	1.61	kilometers
MASS (weight)		
pounds	0.45	kilograms
tons	0.91	metric tons
VOLUME		
cubic yards	0.77	cubic meters
TEMPERATURE		
degrees Fahrenheit	0.56 (*after* subtracting 32)	degrees Celsius

In recognition of South Korea's rapid modernization, the International Olympic Committee chose the nation's capital city of Seoul to host the 1988 summer Olympics. At the opening ceremonies for the games, a torch procession passed through Seoul's South Gate, which dates from the fifteenth century.

Introduction

South Korea—a small nation located on a peninsula between China and Japan—is an economic leader among Asian countries. Because it has developed many industries since the 1960s, South Korea can compete in world trade. This success comes despite the destruction the nation experienced during the Korean War (1950–1953). The conflict pitted newly independent South Korea against neighboring Communist North Korea.

The two Koreas were a single land during much of their history. At times, foreign governments have ruled the peninsula, which served as a land bridge linking Japanese and Chinese cultures. From 1910 to 1945, for example, Korea was a Japanese colony. In 1945, when the Soviet Union and the United States defeated Japan in World War II, they divided the Korean Peninsula. The two world powers were supposed to decide when the Koreans were ready to be

7

From the tenth to the fourteenth centuries, Korean artists were famed for their celadons—bluish green pieces of porcelain. The works, which are highly prized, are imitated by contemporary potters. This celadon incense burner is seven inches high.

reunified under their own government. But the philosophies of the Soviet Union and the United States conflicted, and disagreement grew about how the peninsula should operate. Korea has remained divided ever since, with a Soviet-supported Communist state in the north and a U.S.-supported capitalist nation in the south.

The division of the peninsula separated millions of South Koreans from their relatives in the north. With the same ethnic background, North and South Koreans share a cultural and historical identity. These ties have kept alive a strong desire among Koreans on both sides to reunify the peninsula. Indeed, in recent years masses of South Korean youths have gathered frequently to urge their government to open reunification talks. But the two nations have followed very different paths since the Korean War, making reunification a difficult goal to achieve.

After the division of the Korean Peninsula in 1945, many Koreans in the north fled south to escape the Communist government set up by the Soviet Union in North Korea. Here, members of a refugee family carrying all of their possessions approach the Military Demarcation Line between North and South Korea.

Rice—South Korea's principal crop—thrives in the country's fertile lowlands.

1) The Land

Located on the southern half of a peninsula in eastern Asia, South Korea has rugged mountains and fertile river valleys. Almost completely surrounded by water, the country averages about 150 miles in width and extends 230 miles south toward Honshu, the main island of Japan. South Korea's total land area is 38,022 square miles, making it slightly smaller than the state of Virginia. Numerous islands dot over 750 miles of South Korean coastline.

Three principal bodies of water wash against South Korea's shores. To the west is the Hwang (Yellow) Sea, which separates the country from China. To the east between Korea and Japan lies the Sea of Japan, which the Koreans call the East Sea. To the south is the East China Sea, or South Sea, which contains Cheju, the largest offshore island. The 120-mile-wide Korea Strait connects the East China Sea to the Sea of Japan.

The nation's only land boundary is with North Korea. The Military Demarcation Line has separated the two Koreas since the close of the Korean War in 1953. A Demilitarized Zone patrolled by U.S.- and Soviet-supported armies extends 1.25 miles on each side of the border. Because North and South Korea hope to eventually reunify the peninsula, both nations regard the line as temporary.

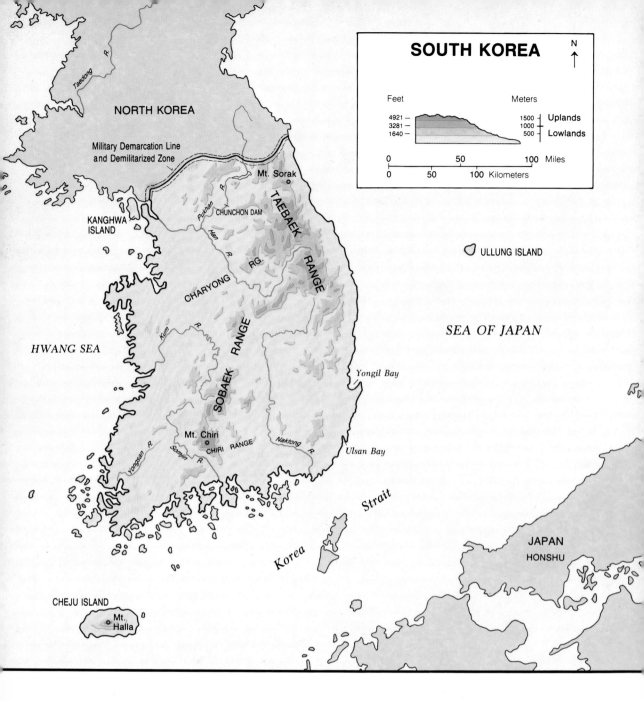

Topography

The eastern coast of South Korea forms a nearly straight line, with few islands and only two natural harbors—Yongil and Ulsan bays. In contrast, the southern and western coasts are jagged and irregular, with many islands, peninsulas, and bays. The difference in the shape of the shorelines is due to geologic movement beneath the ocean. The eastern coast is gradually rising, while the southern and western shores are sinking.

The shifting of the earth's crust under the ocean floor has made eastern and central South Korea mountainous, with rocky cliffs dropping into the Sea of Japan. In the south and west, hills and valleys gradually slope down to the sea, and the shores

Numerous fishing villages dot South Korea's coastline.

Courtesy of Korea National Tourism Corporation

contain lowland plains. Although elevations are not extremely high anywhere in the country, mountains are the main feature of the landscape.

Extending throughout most of eastern and central South Korea, low mountains cover about 70 percent of the country. The Taebaek and Sobaek ranges run from north to south, and the Charyong and Chiri mountains follow an east-west direction. Mount Sorak (5,604 feet) in the Taebaek Range is noted for its scenic beauty, and Mount Chiri (6,283 feet) is the highest peak in peninsular South Korea. Farmers cultivate some land in the mountains, but forests cover most of the area. More than one-fourth of South Korea's population lives in this mountainous region.

Courtesy of Korea National Tourism Corporation

Brilliant colors draw visitors to Mount Sorak National Park in autumn.

Lowlands, which lie primarily along the southern and western coasts, make up about 30 percent of South Korea's territory. Rolling hills and plains characterize the lowlands, and farmers grow most of the nation's crops in this region. Almost one-fourth of the South Korean people live in the southern plain, and approximately half reside along the western coast—especially around Seoul, the nation's capital and principal industrial area.

Numerous islands, which are actually the tips of submerged mountains, fringe the southern and western coasts of South Korea. People inhabit the largest of these islands—including Cheju, Ullung, and Kanghwa. Cheju Island lies about 50 miles south of the peninsula and covers 700 square miles. Rising from the island is Mount Halla, South Korea's tallest peak (6,398 feet). As the largest island, Cheju has its own provincial government, but provinces on the mainland administer the other islands.

Rivers

South Korea's major rivers flow south or west, emptying into the Korea Strait or the Hwang Sea. Most of these waterways are broad and shallow, and the volume they carry varies widely between rainy and dry seasons. The streams that flow east into the Sea of Japan are short, straight, and fast. Important sources of irrigation, South Korea's rivers water more than 70 percent of the nation's rice fields. Large dams help to control flooding during the rainy season. They also produce hydroelectricity and regulate water for domestic and industrial uses.

South Korea's longest river, the 325-mile Naktong, rises in the Taebaek Range and flows south, emptying into the Korea Strait at the city of Pusan. The Han River also begins in the Taebaek mountains and travels west for 318 miles before entering the Hwang Sea. Other major rivers include the Kum, the Somjin, and the Yongsan.

Climate

Seasonal winds called monsoons affect South Korea's weather. During the summer months (June through September), a monsoon from the south and southeast brings hot, humid air to the country. Cold, dry weather comes with a monsoon from the north and northwest during the winter (December through March). Because the mountains shield the eastern coast from the northwest monsoon, this coastal

Courtesy of Korea National Tourism Corporation

Hundreds of rocky islets fringe the Korean Peninsula.

The Chunchon Dam on the Pukhan River—a tributary of the Han—generates electric power for the surrounding region.

region experiences warmer winters than the rest of the country does. Summer temperatures hover around 77° F throughout South Korea. The average temperature in January in Seoul is about 23° F. The winter weather in the capital city is 15 to 20 degrees colder than it is along the southern coast.

South Korea receives about 40 inches of precipitation per year. About half of the

Snow blankets the mountains of South Korea in winter.

13

Cherry blossoms signal the arrival of spring in the South Korean countryside.

rain falls between June and August. Precipitation levels can vary widely, however, and serious droughts occur about once every eight years. A few typhoons (Pacific hurricanes) usually pass over South Korea in late summer, bringing strong winds and heavy rains that damage crops and homes.

Flora and Fauna

The Korean Peninsula and its islands support many different plants. Forests contain pine trees and deciduous (leafshedding) hardwoods such as maple, birch, poplar, oak, ash, and elm. Varieties of fruit trees include apple, pear, peach, apricot, plum, persimmon, and Chinese quince.

Above the timberline (beyond which trees cannot grow), the highest mountains support only alpine vegetation—that is, plants that can survive high altitudes and cold temperatures. In the southern coastal regions, subtropical plants such as orange and other citrus trees thrive. The richest variety of plant life is found on the warm southern islands. Cheju, for example, has

The rose of Sharon, South Korea's national flower, blooms on a small, shrubby tree native to Asia.

more than 70 species of broad-leaved evergreens, while the southern coast of the peninsula has less than 20 species.

July, the hottest month, is the peak period for blooming plants. The number of flowering species in a given region is smaller in areas where the temperature is lower. Camellias blossom all year in the warmest places. The rose of Sharon, South Korea's national flower, blooms from late spring to early fall.

At one time, the forests of South Korea supported many large mammals, including tigers, leopards, lynx, bears, and deer. These animals have become increasingly rare in recent decades, however, as humans have developed areas that were once wild. Smaller mammals include weasels, badgers, and marten. The goral—a cross between a goat and an antelope—inhabits mountainous areas.

About 370 species of birds exist in South Korea. Of these, about 50 types live in the region year-round. The ring-necked pheasant, a bird often hunted in South Korea, inhabits the open countryside. Other wildlife includes several kinds of reptiles and amphibians, as well as freshwater fish.

Courtesy of Korean Overseas Information Services

Herons *(above)* **have long been a favorite subject of Korean poems and paintings. The white, graceful wading birds are traditionally considered a symbol of purity. An eighteenth-century painting** *(right)* **portrays the now-extinct Korean tiger, which ancient Koreans worshiped as a messenger of mountain spirits. Few large mammals still exist in South Korea.**

Courtesy of Korean Overseas Information Services

15

Courtesy of Korean Overseas Information Services

One of the most densely populated countries in the world, South Korea faces many urban challenges.

Cities

With a population of over 9.6 million, South Korea's capital of Seoul is one of the 10 largest cities in the world. Home to nearly one-fourth of the nation's people, Seoul is situated on the Han River about 20 miles east of the Hwang Sea. The city serves as the cultural, economic, educational, and governmental center of the nation. Inchon (population 1.4 million), a

seaport at the mouth of the Han River, handles much of Seoul's shipping.

For more than 500 years, Seoul was the capital of the Korean Choson dynasty (family of rulers). The city expanded and modernized rapidly under Japanese rule from 1910 to 1945. Although the Korean War destroyed much of Seoul, it has been largely rebuilt since the war ended in 1953. Some historical structures still stand amid modern skyscrapers. As evidence of its growing international importance, Seoul hosted the summer Olympic Games in 1988.

Pusan (population 3.5 million) is South Korea's second largest city and largest port. Located in the southeast on the Korea Strait, Pusan is the hub of South Korea's fishing industry, as well as an administrative, commercial, and industrial center. With beaches, hot springs, and historical landmarks, the city attracts many tourists.

About 50 miles northwest of Pusan on the Naktong River lies Taegu (population 2 million), South Korea's third largest urban center. Landmarks in Taegu include the Talsong Fortress, which ancient rulers built over 3,000 years ago. Taegu—the nation's largest producer of textiles—is a regional commercial and educational hub. Other large communities in South Korea—such as Kwangju, Taejon, and Chonju—are provincial capitals that serve as local marketplaces and administrative centers.

Athletic and housing facilities built in Seoul for the 1988 summer Olympics have since relieved some of the population pressures in the capital city.

The port facilities at Pusan on South Korea's southern coast handle the largest percentage of the nation's trade.

Taegu, an industrial center and market town for local farmers, is large enough to offer many urban conveniences but small enough to have a more relaxed atmosphere than that of Seoul or Pusan.

Throughout Cheju Island, *tolharu-bang,* or grandfather stones, can be found. Carved from volcanic lava, these ancient statues may represent legendary guardians that once stood at the entrances to the island's largest townships. The figures resemble sculptures found in other parts of South Korea and on some Pacific islands, such as Tahiti, Okinawa, Fiji, and Easter Island.

2) History and Government

Although Koreans have had long periods of stable self-government, they have lived at times under rule from China, Mongolia, Japan, the Soviet Union, and the United States. Despite centuries of foreign control, however, Koreans have maintained a distinct cultural and political identity.

Archaeologists have uncovered stone tools on the Korean Peninsula that are estimated to be 30,000 years old. Scholars know little about the earliest inhabitants of the region. Finds that date from around 4000 B.C., however, reveal much information about prehistoric Koreans. These people probably migrated from Siberia (now in the Soviet Union), Mongolia (in east central Asia), and Manchuria (now in northeastern China).

As hunters, fishermen, and farmers, the early Koreans worshiped nature gods and ancestral spirits, following a belief system called shamanism. These religious practices remained strong even after the introduction of Buddhism, Confucianism, and Christianity in later centuries.

Ancient Choson

According to popular legend, a leader named Tangun founded Korea in 2333 B.C. by uniting several ethnic groups into one kingdom. Tangun is said to be the son of a heavenly prince and a bear that was transformed into a maiden. Called Ancient Choson, the realm that Tangun established lasted more than 1,000 years.

Centered in the northwestern corner of the Korean Peninsula, Choson also spread north and west beyond the peninsula. In the twelfth century B.C., the northern

19

A painting from the sixth-century Tomb of the Dancers depicts a hunting scene during the reign of the Koguryo dynasty.

Chinese state of Yan began to increase its power and prevented Choson from further expansion. Eventually, the Yan invaded Choson. In the third century B.C., the invaders took over territory west of the Liao River to the northwest of the Korean Peninsula.

Gradually Ancient Choson split into smaller units. In southern Korea, the states of Mahan, Chinhan, and Pyonhan arose. The Han dynasty of China conquered northern Korea in 109 B.C. and established four colonies—Luolang, Zhenfan, Xuantu, and Lintun. The Chinese, however, soon lost their authority in all of the colonies except Luolang, and local leagues ran the area. Nevertheless, Chinese influence on the Korean Peninsula remained strong for 400 years, and Chinese models shaped the civilization and government of the region.

The Three Kingdoms

During the second century A.D., several Korean groups united and formed the state of Koguryo in the northeastern part of the peninsula. Despite repeated attacks by the Chinese, Koguryo gained control of a portion of Manchuria east of the Liao River. The state also extended across the northern and central parts of the Korean Peninsula. In A.D. 313, Koguryo finally ousted the Chinese from Luolang.

Large Korean states were slower to develop south of the Han River, perhaps because the area was more isolated. The region's people did not initially need to unite because direct Chinese control did not threaten them. By about the mid-200s, however, inhabitants of the southern portion of the peninsula began to fear foreign domination. This concern caused two kingdoms—Silla and Paekche—to develop. Divided by the Sobaek Range, the two realms had little contact with each other.

In the southwest the Paekche kingdom arose after Luolang threatened the region in A.D. 245. The Silla kingdom evolved in the southeast. At first, a few groups on the south central tip of the peninsula—known as Kaya—maintained ties with Japan rather than joining either Paekche or Silla. In time, however, these two kingdoms absorbed the independent groups.

Each of the three kingdoms adopted Buddhism, a religion that had been founded in India in the sixth century B.C. Koguryo accepted the new faith first, in A.D. 372, and Paekche followed in 384. Silla did not make Buddhism its official religion until 528. The Chinese brought Buddhist scriptures to the Korean Peninsula. The visitors also introduced Confucianism—the ideas of the Chinese philosopher Confucius—which taught ethical behavior and respect for authority.

When Koguryo began to expand in the 500s and 600s, it came into conflict with the Sui dynasty of China to the west and with Silla to the south. Koguryo repelled the Sui forces. Silla leaders, however, allied themselves with the Chinese Tang dynasty. Silla and Tang forces overcame Paekche, Koguryo's ally, in 660. They went on to conquer Koguryo in 668. Famines and internal strife in Koguryo contributed to the northern kingdom's defeat.

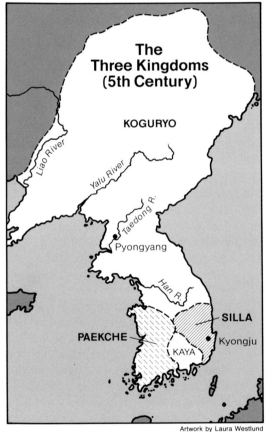

The Three Kingdoms (5th Century)

KOGURYO

Liao River

Yalu River

Taedong R.

Pyongyang

Han R.

SILLA

PAEKCHE

KAYA

Kyongju

Artwork by Laura Westlund

This map shows the boundaries of the three kingdoms of Koguryo, Silla, and Paekche in the fifth century. Silla and Paekche would later absorb the Kaya region. After the three kingdoms were united in 668, the unified Silla realm encompassed the Korean Peninsula up to the Taedong River.

Independent Picture Service

An artist crafted this golden crown for Silla royalty in the fifth century.

After Silla unified the Korean Peninsula, its own existence was threatened by its former ally, the Tang dynasty. Silla successfully resisted Chinese rule on most of the peninsula, but it lost the Koguryo territory north of the Taedong River. With most of the Korean Peninsula under its control, the unified Silla kingdom developed a society and culture that shaped much of Korea's later history.

Silla Dynasty

Silla power reached its peak in the mid-eighth century, when rulers sought to create the ideal Buddhist state. Buddhist art and architecture thrived during this period. The government hired diplomats, doctors, mathematicians, and astronomers. A new program distributed land more equally among peasants, and in return they gave rice, millet, barley, and wheat to the government. They also raised silkworms and walnut and pine-nut trees, whose products went to Silla officials and other wealthy people.

Silla's capital city at Kyongju prospered. A few high-positioned residents, however, enjoyed a comfortable life at the expense of common people, who often worked as slaves. The "bone-rank" system—a social structure based on bloodlines—gave a small group of people more importance than the rest of the population.

In the ninth century, the rich led an easy, luxurious lifestyle that violated the teachings of Buddhism. As a result, the role of Buddhism as the state religion began to weaken. Furthermore, conflict arose among various wealthy families who

Courtesy of Korean Overseas Information Services

The kings and queens of Silla were buried in huge earthen mounds in Kyongju, the dynasty's capital. Ceramics and objects crafted from gold and silver—such as jewelry, crowns, belts, and goblets—have been found in the tombs.

Pulguksa, a temple complex about 10 miles east of Kyongju, is among the oldest surviving Buddhist monasteries in South Korea. One of the best examples of Silla-era architecture, Pulguksa was first built in the early fifth century. The complex has undergone various additions and restorations since then.

sought to gain the throne or the administration of a district for themselves.

By 900, rebel Korean leaders had split Silla apart, reestablishing the kingdoms of Paekche and Koguryo. During the next several decades, these three realms fought for control of the Korean Peninsula. In 935 Wang Kon, the leader of Later Koguryo, conquered Later Paekche, and he absorbed Silla the following year. By leaving outlying districts undisturbed and by befriending Silla's rich class, Wang Kon secured his rule. He gave Silla's former king, Kyongsun, the highest position in the

Made of gold-plated bronze, this Maitreya, or Buddha of the Future, is considered one of South Korea's national treasures. The figure is about 2.5 feet high and dates from the early seventh century.

23

Sokkuram, a cave temple near Pulguksa, contains a white granite image of Buddha that is nearly 12 feet in height. Two menacing guards protect the entrance to the inner chamber. Made of granite, the artificial cave is covered with earth to blend into a hillside.

government, and he married a woman from the Silla royal family.

The Koryo Kingdom

Under Wang Kon, the Korean Peninsula was under the control of a single kingdom once again. Wang Kon named the region Koryo, from which the word *Korea* is derived. He extended the state's northern boundary to the Yalu River, where Koryo forces fought with Manchurian troops from 993 to 1018. Koryo maintained its position and established peace with Manchuria in 1022.

Koryo culture peaked in the eleventh century, when the kingdom's rulers borrowed Chinese political and economic systems. Buddhism inspired scholarly work and art. The ceramics industry produced prized celadons—pottery with a

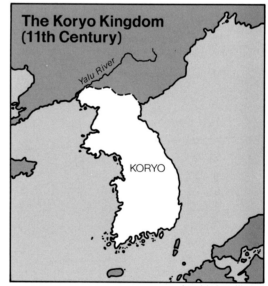

The Koryo Kingdom (11th Century)

Yalu River

KORYO

The leader Wang Kon extended the northern border of Koryo to the Yalu River at the northern end of the Korean Peninsula.

24

bluish green glaze. The rise of printing in China encouraged the Koryo dynasty to pursue printing and publication, and in 1234 Koreans invented the world's first movable metal type.

In the twelfth century, Koryo's stability began to crumble. Powerful aristocratic families struggled with the king for political control. In 1170 military leaders rebelled, frustrated that they did not rank as highly as did other government officials. Soldiers seized power, and later kings were only symbolic rulers with little authority.

Meanwhile, the Mongols to the north invaded Koryo in 1231, and they soon overcame the kingdom. The Mongol emperor Kublai Khan enlisted Koreans in his expeditions against Japan. The Japanese, who were aided by seasonal typhoons, repelled the weather-beaten Mongolian

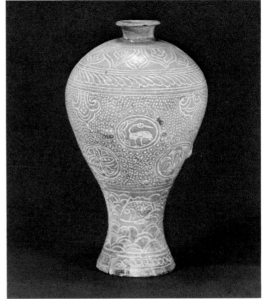

Photo by Museum of Fine Arts, Boston

The Koryo period is famed for its delicate, intricately patterned celadons.

Courtesy of Korean Overseas Information Services

Buddhist monks took 16 years to carve over 80,000 wooden printing blocks for the *Tripitaka Koreana,* a book of Buddhist scriptures. Begun in 1235, the sacred project was undertaken to seek divine aid to ward off the invading Mongols. The blocks have been carefully preserved against deterioration at Haein-sa Temple.

Courtesy of Korean Overseas Information Services

This 10-story stone pagoda (temple) was built during the late Koryo period and is located on the grounds of Kyongbok Palace in Seoul.

forces. Koryo, however, remained under Mongolian domination until 1368, when the Chinese Ming dynasty pushed the Mongols back to the north.

After 1350, Japanese pirates began to attack the Korean coast more frequently than they had in the past. Yi Song-gye, a Koryo military commander, defeated the raiders in a series of battles. He also gained influence in Koryo's internal affairs, which were politically unstable.

Koryo's leaders could not agree on whether to favor ties with the Ming or ties with the Mongols. Yi Song-gye supported friendly relations with the Ming. When the king of Koryo ordered Yi to attack Ming forces on the Liaodong Peninsula, the general revolted. Turning his army against the capital, Yi seized the throne in 1392 and founded the Choson (or Yi) dynasty, which lasted until the early 1900s.

Choson Dynasty

During the Koryo dynasty, powerful clans and Buddhist monasteries had come to control large portions of farmland. The landowners collected a high percentage of crops as rent from peasants who worked the land. Yi made many reforms to gain the support of the peasants, who formed most of the population. He ordered huge acreages to be stripped from the landlords and reclaimed the land for the government. In this way, the Choson dynasty increased its own income while easing the hardships of tenant farmers. In control of the land—the nation's wealth—was the *yangban* class. The yangban were a group of scholar-officials who were educated in Confucian thought.

For the Buddhist monasteries, the loss of these estates meant the loss of economic and political power. Choson leaders denounced Buddhism as a corrupt institution and upheld Confucianism as the ideal model for Korean society. With the decline of Buddhism, Korea became a primarily secular (nonreligious) society, since Confu-

26

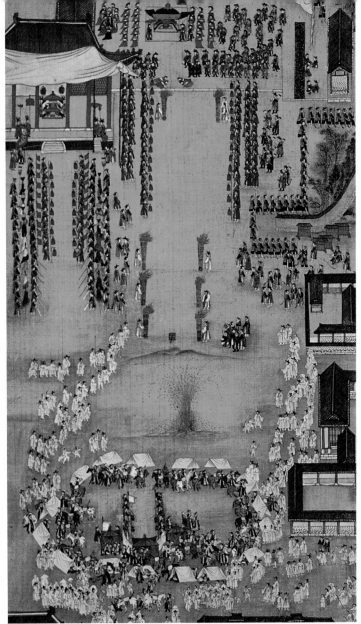

A painted screen depicts a royal procession during the Choson dynasty. This family of rulers widely supported Chinese Confucian practices in Korea. Respect for authority and a clear-cut social and political order were important elements in the Confucian state.

cianism was a system of ethics rather than a religion.

The greatest Choson ruler was King Sejong, the fourth monarch, who reigned from 1418 to 1450. Sejong fostered the arts, science, and technology. The invention of the Korean alphabet in 1446 made written information available to more Koreans. Tax reforms and health measures improved the lives of the people.

After Sejong, however, Korea fell into the hands of less able rulers. Succession to the throne often caused bitter struggles, and members of the yangban competed for power. Corruption became widespread as royal relatives and powerful factions increased their landholdings and kept the taxes they collected for themselves. These groups further burdened farmers by raising taxes and rents.

Foreign invasions made Korea's internal problems worse. Attacks from the Japanese in 1592 and 1597 and from the Chinese in 1627 and 1636 upset the economy

27

Courtesy of Korean Overseas Information Services

Near Toksu Palace in Seoul, a statue commemorates King Sejong, the father of the Korean alphabet.

Courtesy of Korean Overseas Information Services

A painting portrays the lodge of the artist Chong Son, who worked for the Choson dynasty. Known as the Hermit Village for Retirement, the lodge provided a secluded retreat where scholars could study and meditate.

and ruined much farmland. Koreans drove the Japanese off the peninsula, but the Chinese armies were stronger than the Koreans. Although the Choson dynasty continued to rule, the state sent tribute (payments) to the Chinese emperor until the late nineteenth century.

Social and Economic Upheaval

During the seventeenth and eighteenth centuries, new social and economic conditions enabled the general population to change Choson society. Merchants became important, and, as the economy grew, money replaced barter in many commercial transactions. As merchants became wealthy, the aristocracy became less powerful, and Koreans were able to improve their social status more easily. Writers began to describe a society that valued equality and justice.

Two schools of thought during this period reflected the social changes. One was *Sirhak,* or "practical learning," which emphasized finding realistic solutions to Choson's social and economic problems. Sirhak scholars had little patience for the

Courtesy of Korean Overseas Information Services

Korean soldiers defend the port of Pusan against a 1590s Japanese invasion in this period artwork.

traditional Confucian models that Choson rulers had followed for centuries. They felt that the abstract ideas of Confucianism did not apply to Korean society. A new interest in science and Western technology helped to shape the Sirhak movement.

The second intellectual influence—made up of Western scientific and religious ideas —came to Choson by way of China. Choson officials had closed their country to all foreigners except the Chinese, hoping to keep out disruptive new influences. China, however, absorbed European ideas, which in turn affected Choson. Western science and technology gained the respect of some scholars in Korea, who felt that scientific knowledge would benefit Korean society.

In addition, Roman Catholicism, which Portuguese missionaries brought to China, attracted some Koreans. Catholics taught that equality and eternal salvation were the rights of everyone. These beliefs matched newly aroused Korean goals but clashed with the traditional Korean social order. Choson officials outlawed Catholicism because the religion opposed ancestor worship and rigid social classes.

The economic and social developments that began in the 1600s and 1700s

Hyangwonjong—a six-sided, two-story pavilion—rises on an artificial island in a large lagoon at Seoul's Kyongbok Palace.

Photo by David Tykol

continued during the early 1800s. An ongoing struggle for power among rival officials thwarted political reform, but numerous peasant revolts gradually led to some improvements in the conditions of farmers.

A leader named Choe Che-u formed the ideas of a new movement called *Tonghak,* or "eastern learning." His philosophy was intended to rescue farmers from poverty and unrest and to restore political and social stability. Tonghak combined elements of Eastern thought—such as Con-

Historically, lower-class residents of the Korean Peninsula used masked dances to criticize the aristocracy. Originating as religious drama, these dances became a means of portraying corrupt monks, rude *yangban* (scholar-officials), greedy merchants, scolding housewives, and quack witch doctors. Song, dance, pantomime, comic dialogue, colorful costumes, and expressive masks were all part of the performance.

Courtesy of Korean Overseas Information Services

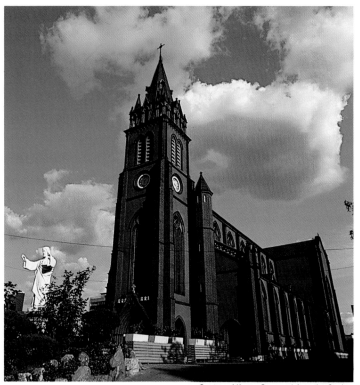

Myongdong Cathedral, which was built in 1898, still stands in Seoul as testimony to the continuing influence of Christianity in Korea.

Courtesy of Korean Overseas Information Services

The Sokchon ceremony, or Festival of Confucius, honors the spirit of a Korean named Kongja. The principles of this philosopher guided the government and the code of behavior during the Choson dynasty.

fucianism and Buddhism—with modern humanistic thought. Choe set his ideas to music so that farmers who could not read could understand and spread them.

International Involvement

Early in the nineteenth century, British ships entered Korean waters in an attempt to reach new Asian markets. By the 1840s, Russian and French merchants had also entered the region, although the Korean government remained opposed to foreign contact. The Japanese were the first to break Choson's isolation, opening up three Korean ports to Japanese trade in 1876. China, which felt threatened by Japan's advances toward Choson, tried to reestablish its authority in the region. In order to prevent Japan from becoming powerful on the peninsula, China forced Choson to sign treaties with the United States, Britain, Italy, and Russia.

Within Choson, officials split into pro-Chinese, pro-Japanese, and pro-Russian factions. The latter two groups wanted reform and modernization. Still another faction sought independence from any foreign controls. The government, however, quickly curbed nationalist activities be-cause they threatened the Choson dynasty's authority.

In 1894 followers of the Tonghak movement rebelled against the nation's corrupt and oppressive government. The Tonghak Rebellion spread from the southwest to central Choson and the capital at Seoul. When the king of Choson asked Chinese troops to help quell the uprising, the Japanese countered by sending their own forces. The conflict erupted into the Chinese-Japanese War, in which Japan easily defeated both China and the Tonghak rebels.

According to the Treaty of Shimonoseki, which formally ended the war, China gave up the island of Taiwan to Japan, and Choson gained independence from Chinese influence, which had lasted for centuries. The Japanese became involved in Choson's affairs and encouraged various social and political reforms to prevent further internal problems in Choson.

While Japan was extending its control in eastern Asia, Russia had also begun to increase its influence in the region. In addition to taking over parts of northeastern China, Russia claimed a share of Choson's forests and mines. The resulting rivalry between Russia and Japan erupted in the

31

The Tonghak Rebellion of 1894 quickly spread into an international war when both China and Japan, whose interests in Korea conflicted, came to the rescue of the Choson dynasty. Here, Japanese troops defeat the Chinese at the Yalu River.

Russo-Japanese War in 1904, which Japan won. Under the Treaty of Portsmouth, Russia recognized Japan's political, military, and economic interest in Choson. Shortly thereafter Japan made Choson a Japanese protectorate, and on August 22, 1910, Japan annexed Choson as a colony.

Japanese Colonization

After 1910, the Japanese government forced many changes on the Koreans and treated them as a conquered people. The colonizers prevented Koreans from publishing their own newspapers and from organizing political or intellectual groups. Japanese officials tightened control on Korean education, closing nearly 75 percent of all private schools.

In 1919 nationalists seeking Korean independence organized a countrywide uprising known as the March First movement. Although the demonstration did not achieve independence, it marked the beginning of a national awareness that unified all Koreans, regardless of their social class. Throughout the next two decades, Korean

A bronze mural in Seoul's Pagoda Park honors Koreans who demonstrated against Japanese rule during the independence movement of 1919.

resistance to Japanese rule became stronger and more organized. In response, colonial officials increased repression, especially after military leaders gained political power in Japan in the 1930s.

Military power and the thirst for expansion increased in Japan during the 1930s. As a result, Korea became an important military base for Japan's planned invasion of China. Korean youths entered the Japanese army. Colonial rulers encouraged Koreans to replace their loyalty to Korea with allegiance to Japan. One law even required Koreans to worship at Shinto shrines (monuments to the age-old Japanese religion). Japanese officials also urged Koreans to adopt Japanese names. Teachers began to use the Japanese language and covered Japanese subjects.

Japan expanded the Korean economy to prepare for war and to make the Japanese Empire economically independent from the rest of the world. Korea's agricultural base was broadened to meet the Japanese demand for more rice, and large-scale industry grew. Economic growth, however, benefited the Japanese who controlled Korea, not the Koreans. With the outbreak of World War II in the Pacific region in 1941, conditions in Korea worsened. Koreans experienced shortages of food staples such as rice, and Japanese oppression increased.

Partition of Korea

After the defeat of Japan in 1945, the United States and the Soviet Union agreed to divide the Korean Peninsula at the thirty-eighth parallel of latitude. Soviet troops occupied the northern section, and U.S. troops remained in the south.

During the next two years, the two powers worked toward unifying the peninsula —a goal shared by Koreans on both sides of the temporary dividing line. Conferences between the United States and the Soviet Union, however, deteriorated into

Courtesy of Korean Overseas Information Services

On August 15, 1945, at the end of World War II, the residents of Seoul rejoiced at the news of the Japanese surrender and the liberation of Korea.

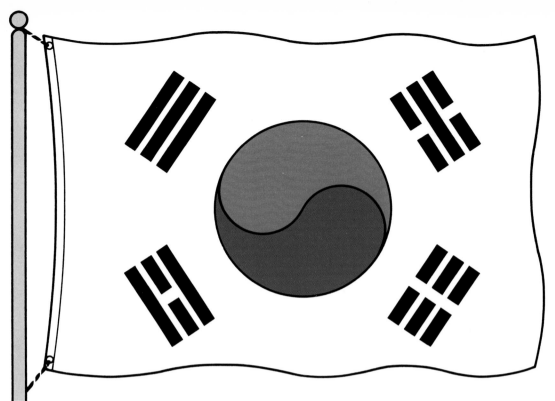

First raised officially in the late nineteenth century, South Korea's flag was adopted in 1950, after the formation of the Republic of Korea. The white field represents the land and peace. The circle is patterned after the *taeguk,* or yin and yang symbol. This image comes from Buddhist philosophy and reflects the opposing forces of nature—such as fire and water, day and night, and male and female. The sets of three broken and unbroken parallel bars are called *kwae.* The upper left kwae denotes the heavens, summer, and the south. The moon, autumn, and the west are represented in the upper right bars. The lower left symbol suggests the earth, winter, and the north. Finally, the sun, spring, and the east are expressed by the kwae in the lower right corner.

mistrust as U.S. and Soviet interests conflicted in other parts of the world.

In 1947 both powers began arranging separate governments for Korea, and the United States submitted the unification problem to the United Nations (UN). The UN offered to supervise elections in Korea to choose one government. When the Soviet Union refused to allow UN representatives into the north, the south held elections alone in 1948.

The south's newly elected national assembly drew up a constitution. In July 1948, Syngman Rhee won the presidential election, and on August 15 the south formed the Republic of Korea. The following month, Communists in the north announced the formation of the Democratic People's Republic of Korea. Both governments claimed to represent all of the Korean Peninsula.

The Korean War

North and South Korean troops clashed along the thirty-eighth parallel several times between 1948 and 1950. Despite this tension, the United States and the Soviet Union withdrew their troops in 1948 and 1949. When U.S. defense forces left the country, North Koreans saw an opportunity to occupy the entire peninsula. On June 25, 1950, Soviet-supplied North Korean troops invaded South Korea.

North Korea ignored the UN's immediate request for them to withdraw from the region. Two days after the invasion, the United States and other members of the

UN sent military forces to South Korea. Initially, the North Koreans took over the entire peninsula up to the Pusan Perimeter—a defensive line about 50 miles from Pusan in the southeast.

On September 15, U.S. soldiers landed at Inchon on the northwestern coast of South Korea. Their surprise arrival, directed by U.S. general Douglas MacArthur, changed the course of the war. The U.S. troops isolated the North Koreans fighting at the Pusan Perimeter from those waging war north of Inchon.

Moving northeast, U.S. forces reached North Korea's northern border along the Yalu River by October 1950. At this time, however, Communist Chinese troops came to North Korea's aid. Within a month, South Korea's army began to retreat, arriving south of Seoul in early 1951. Although the South Koreans regained their capital a few months later, they did not make any other major advances during the remainder of the war.

Truce talks began in July 1951, but fighting continued for two more years before the opposing forces settled on a cease-fire. South Korea gained about 1,500 square miles of territory. A permanent peace treaty has never been signed, and U.S. forces remain in South Korea to discourage open warfare. A 2.5-mile-wide buffer area called the Demilitarized Zone divides the two sides.

The war exacted a huge toll in human lives and in property damage. It also left deep emotional scars on the Korean people, who began to realize that the partition of their homeland would last much longer than they had been led to believe. Since the war, the leaders of both sides have made occasional attempts to discuss reunification. In the mid-1980s, students began to push more strongly for reunification and

The surprise landing of U.S. troops at Inchon during the Korean War required careful timing because the water level changed by 30 feet between high and low tides. Any boat that failed to land at high tide would have been trapped in mud.

To escape Communist forces during the Korean War, a steady stream of refugees from the north traveled south with their belongings.

for the removal of U.S. military bases. Until the north and south can come to trust each other, however, reunification seems unlikely.

Modern Developments

While preparing for World War II, the Japanese had concentrated their industries in the north. As a result, the division of the Korean Peninsula left South Korea with a weak economy. The Korean War aggravated economic problems by destroying crops and factories. Despite President Rhee's failure to improve the economy, voters reelected him in 1952 and 1956.

In the late 1950s, however, Rhee used corrupt methods to remain in control of the government, and his public support dropped. When he won the presidency again in 1960, protesters accused him of rigging the elections and forced him to step down. Newly elected government officials took office in July 1960, but economic difficulties continued, and rival groups began to struggle for political power.

In May 1961, General Park Chung-hee led a military overthrow and took control of the government. Park called for elections to restore democracy, and voters elected him president in 1963. Park quickly reversed South Korea's economy by developing industries and foreign trade.

In 1967 and 1971, Park and his Democratic Republican party won reelection by

In 1965 Park Chung-hee greeted an officer from the U.S. Marines.

a wide margin. He changed the constitution to increase his power and to allow the president to serve an unlimited number of terms. He also altered the election process from direct voting by the people to an electoral system dominated by his own supporters. Park was reelected by the electoral college in 1972 and again in 1978.

After 1972 Park began to limit civil liberties, such as the freedoms of speech, the press, and assembly. He jailed his opponents, claiming that too much criticism might weaken the government and invite attack from North Korea. Park's reign ended abruptly when Kim Jae-gyu, the director of the Korean Central Intelligence Agency, assassinated him in 1979.

Courtesy of Embassy of the Republic of Korea

President Roh Tae-woo waved to supporters during a campaign rally in 1987.

The 1980s

Prime Minister Choi Kyu-ha assumed control of the presidency in 1979, but the military soon took full control of the government. Led by General Chun Doo-hwan, the army thwarted efforts to restore constitutional liberties. Violent clashes between the military and South Korean demonstrators broke out in Kwangju in 1980, and at least 200 people were killed. President Choi resigned the same year, and Chun secured his own election as chief executive. A new constitution limited the president to one seven-year term but maintained strong executive powers.

Although military rule ended in 1981, the Chun government continued to silence those who opposed it. Nevertheless, critics were active and vocal, calling Chun a dictator. Some demonstrations were violent, such as those at Inchon in May 1986 and at Konguk University the following fall. In June 1987, in response to calls for a more democratic constitution, Chun agreed to allow direct election of the president by the people rather than by an electoral college.

In elections held the following December, Roh Tae-woo of Chun's Democratic Justice party received the most votes. Many South Koreans questioned Roh's commitment to democracy because he had participated in the 1979 military coup. Roh's Democratic Justice party was not as successful in elections to the national assembly in the spring of 1988. Because his party failed to win a majority of seats, Roh had to compromise with his opponents in the legislature.

Amid demonstrations calling for his removal from office, Roh sought to improve his image by erasing his connections with the former Chun administration. He gave in to pressure to investigate both the Kwangju massacre of 1980 and corruption during Chun's rule. In 1988 a large student movement began to urge the reunification of North and South Korea, and Roh approached North Korea to open communication between the two governments. Roh's willingness to respond openly to legislative and student opponents is a step in putting South Korea on the road to democracy.

Government

According to the Republic of Korea's Constitution of 1987, executive power belongs to a president, who is directly elected for one five-year term. All South Koreans over

At a student gathering in Seoul in August 1988, a banner urges reunification of North and South Korea.

the age of 19 may vote. Although the constitution guarantees civil rights, such as freedoms of the press and religion, the government can limit these liberties.

The president appoints a prime minister and 15 to 30 state council members, who head government departments and assist the chief executive. The legislature is a one-house national assembly, whose members are elected to four-year terms.

For administrative purposes, South Korea is divided into nine provinces and five cities—Inchon, Kwangju, Pusan, Seoul, and Taegu—that are large enough to rank as provinces. Provinces are further divided into either counties or cities of over 50,000 people. The national government appoints provincial governors, mayors, and other high-ranking local officials.

A supreme court heads South Korea's judicial branch. A chief justice and nine other justices—all of whom are appointed to five-year terms by the president—make up this body. In addition, 3 courts of appeal rehear cases that are still disputed after they have been tried in one of the country's 10 district courts.

In 1953 representatives from North and South Korea signed the cease-fire that halted the Korean War at Panmunjom. The site lies 35 miles north of Seoul in the heavily patrolled Demilitarized Zone. Visitors can view North Korea from the observation deck at Panmunjom but are not permitted to cross the border. Military meetings and occasional reunification talks are held in buildings that straddle the Military Demarcation Line. The tight control in the Demilitarized Zone and the dead-end results of talks held so far calls to question hopes for reunification.

The *Nong-ak,* or Farmer's Dance, has been popular among Koreans for centuries to stimulate work and to celebrate agricultural events such as planting and harvesting. In recent years, the dance has also been used as a reminder of the importance of promoting agriculture as well as industry. The inscription on one of the banners reads, "Farmers are the Principals of the World." Performed to the loud accompaniment of gongs and drums, the Nong-ak is energetic and colorful.

3) The People

South Korea, one of the most densely populated countries in the world, has about 42.6 million people. Because much of the country is mountainous, the population is squeezed into the plains along the western coast and along the nation's many streams and rivers. Sixty-five percent of the people live in urban areas. To curb its rapidly growing population, which has little room for expansion, the government started a program in 1962 to limit the average family size. Seventy percent of South Korean women now use some form of birth control,

and the nation has cut its growth rate in half.

Very few foreigners live in South Korea. Of these, the Chinese make up the largest minority. Although South Koreans are a single people who share a common physical appearance, language, and culture, their exact ethnic origins are uncertain. Most scholars believe that South Koreans are descendants of nomadic peoples from Mongolia. The Korean racial type probably developed before the beginning of the first century A.D. Contact with the Chinese

39

Courtesy of Korean Overseas Information Services

Children traditionally bow to parents and elders during New Year's rituals. Respect for elders remains an important element in South Korean family life.

ture supported by Confucian ideas. Members of the upper classes learned Confucian classics and studied correct social behavior. The commoners, who formed a huge majority of the population, were small-scale farmers, agricultural workers, merchants, craftspeople, and slaves. Most important in the social organization was the family unit, or clan.

Family Life

Traditionally, the Korean family revolved around the father, supported itself economically, and conformed to the Confucian social order. Families historically provided individual members with money, social rank, and far-reaching connections that included distant relatives. Family line and position within this unit determined an individual's place in society. The family, therefore, was valued more than the individual.

throughout later centuries left little influence on the physical appearance of the Koreans.

The South Korean way of life draws on ancient customs as as well as on modern, Westernized styles. In large cities, many people have adopted Western dress and Western ideas. In the countryside the way of life stays more or less as it has been for thousands of years. When Western influence first entered Korea in the seventeenth century, the nation had a rigid social struc-

Status within the family was based primarily on generation, age, and gender. The relationship between father and son held the most importance, since the son would head the family after his father's death. Women held the lowest positions. In some cases, particularly among the wealthy, a household included not only a husband, a wife, and their children but also grandparents, aunts, uncles, and cousins.

Courtesy of Korean Overseas Information Services

On special occasions, several Korean dishes are served at once, completely filling the table.

Traditional Korean houses are often L-shaped structures with tile roofs.

Although the family is still the most important unit in Korean society, its form and function are changing. Respect for elders remains, as do elaborate weddings and funerals, family responsibility for the welfare of members, and favoritism because of family ties. Most South Koreans, however, no longer depend on the family to care for distant relatives. Urban households usually consist of the immediate family, without extended members. Older customs are still followed on some family farms.

Weddings in rural areas are usually traditional affairs for which parents make all the arrangements, including choosing a mate for their child. In contrast, young people living in cities often pick their own marriage partners, sometimes without the consent of their parents. Modern couples may rent wedding halls—facilities that are equipped with music, flowers, and Western-styled bridal gowns and formal suits.

Food and Housing

Rice, cooked alone or with other grains, is the main food at all Korean meals. Various side dishes—such as bean-paste soup, kimchi (pickled vegetables), steamed and seasoned vegetables, roast beef, and fish—accompany the rice. Soy sauce, soybean paste, red pepper, ginger root, and sesame oil and seeds add flavor to Korean foods. A favorite dish is *pulgogi,* which is beef strips marinated in a mixture of soy sauce, sesame oil and seeds, pepper, onion, and garlic and broiled over a charcoal fire. *Shinsollo* combines meat, eggs, nuts, and vegetables in an artistic arrangement.

Traditional Korean homes are one-story structures made of brick or concrete blocks and roofed with tiles, slate, or corrugated zinc. Most of these houses have a living room, a kitchen, and a bedroom. A heating system called *ondol* provides warmth to South Korean homes. In such a system, stone pipes under the floor carry hot air from the kitchen fire. Almost all South Korean homes have electricity.

Religion

South Korea's constitution guarantees complete religious freedom for its people, and historically Koreans have been tolerant of various faiths. Many South Koreans borrow practices from more than one

41

set of beliefs. The major religions found in South Korea are Buddhism, Confucianism, Christianity, and shamanism.

Shamanism, the oldest belief system on the Korean Peninsula, is based on the worship of nature. According to shamanism, the universe and everything in it are sacred, and each part—the sun, mountains, rocks, and trees, for example—contains a spirit. Some Koreans consult shamans (priests) to cure illness or to control events. Shamanism teaches that unwell people are possessed by a spirit and that only a shaman can release this spirit by performing a *kut*—a ritual composed of dances, songs, and prayers.

Confucianism and Buddhism were both introduced to the Korean Peninsula from China between the fourth and seventh centuries A.D. In general, Buddhists believe that they can achieve peace and happiness by rejecting their attachment to worldly things and by leading a life of virtue and wisdom. Very few people have ever reached this goal, and those who have are referred to as Buddhas, or "Enlightened Ones." The birthday of Gautama Buddha, who founded the faith in India in the sixth century B.C., is a national holiday in South Korea.

Buddhism strongly influenced Koreans until the fifteenth century. At that time,

This landscape is part of a painted screen that was placed behind the throne of Choson rulers during the eighteenth century. The image contains the sacred elements of nature with which humans should be in harmony. Although unspoiled natural settings are diminishing in number, many South Koreans still honor nature.

South Korean Buddhists *(left)* pray and make offerings on Buddha's birthday, a national holiday. Shaman totem poles *(below)* ward off evil spirits.

the Choson dynasty (1392–1910) replaced Buddhism with Confucianism as the state religion. A Chinese philosophy, Confucianism sets forth ethical concepts to guide behavior. These guidelines assume that there are no divine beings to influence good conduct.

Christianity first entered Korea by way of China in the 1600s. Catholic missionaries arrived in 1785, and Protestants came in the 1880s. Although the government persecuted missionaries, in part because Christians were intolerant of other religions, the faith gained many converts. At the close of the 1980s, about 16 percent of the South Korean people followed Christianity.

Many South Koreans perform rites to worship their ancestors, one of the most important duties in Confucianism.

During the nineteenth and twentieth centuries, South Koreans who believe that the modern world is meaningless and morally weak have practiced so-called new religions. Established by people who claim to have received a message from a god, these new faiths draw from Christianity as well as from the traditional religions of Korea.

With improved health conditions in South Korea, more babies are surviving the first year of life and more people are entering old age.

Health

Rapid economic growth since the early 1960s has improved the living conditions and therefore the health of South Koreans. A life expectancy that stood at 52 years in the late 1950s had risen to 68 by 1989. During the same period, the number of infants who died in the first year of life had decreased to 30 out of every 1,000 live births—a figure that is significantly lower than the Asian average of 96 per 1,000.

Nevertheless, some health problems remain. Poor sanitation—including inadequate sewage systems and contaminated water—threatens both urban and rural populations. Industries and agricultural fertilizers have polluted the land and water. Seoul and other major cities have begun to tackle these unhealthy conditions.

In the early 1980s, the main causes of death were respiratory diseases—such as tuberculosis, bronchitis, and pneumonia—and illnesses of the stomach and intestines. More efficient agricultural methods and contact with world food markets have improved South Korean nutrition in recent decades.

Although urban medical facilities are well developed, the government is still striving to extend full health care to rural areas. A medical insurance program that began in 1977 benefits over half of South Korea's people, and the government hopes to extend coverage to the entire population by the year 2000.

Education

Until the late nineteenth century, only the sons of wealthy families attended school. At the end of the 1800s, Christian missionaries started schools that offered education to a broader portion of the population, including women.

Under Japanese rule from 1910 to 1945, the school system taught Japanese culture as well as technical courses that prepared Koreans for work in an industrialized society. But the Japanese severely limited educational opportunities for Koreans by closing private schools and by strictly controlling state-run institutions. Many Koreans remained illiterate during this period. After World War II, South Korea faced the task of building an educational system to fit a modern industrialized society.

In the 1950s, the South Korean government established the Ministry of Education, an office that controls courses, funding, enrollment quotas, and other administrative matters. Schools also resumed teaching in the Korean language. The nation's literacy rate jumped from 22 percent in 1945 to 92 percent in 1989, demonstrating the success of the government's educational policies.

Six years of primary school are free of charge and compulsory. More than 98 percent of South Korean children between the ages of 6 and 12 attend elementary classes. Almost all of these students complete three additional years of middle school. Ninety percent of the South Korean people participate in the three-year high school program. Institutes of higher learning include four-year colleges and universities and two-year junior and vocational colleges. About 36 percent of all high-school graduates enroll in postsecondary institutions.

Students at a South Korean school listen attentively to their teacher.

Language

Most experts group the Korean language with other tongues that originated in the Altai Mountains of central Asia. This group also includes the Mongolian, Turkish, and Finnish languages. As a result of Chinese cultural influence throughout much of Korea's history, the Korean language borrows more than 50 percent of its vocabulary from Chinese. The official language used in South Korea is modeled on the dialect spoken around Seoul. Although other dialects are spoken in other regions of the country, South Koreans can easily understand all of them except for the version used on Cheju Island.

Hangul, the Korean alphabet, consists of 10 vowels and 14 consonants that are arranged in syllables rather than in words. Developed during the reign of King Sejong in the fifteenth century, hangul is considered to be one of the most logical writing

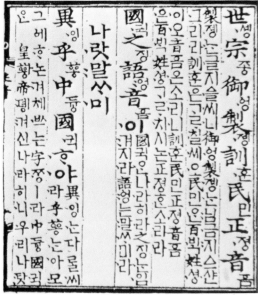

Courtesy of Korean Overseas Information Services

A page from *Hunmin-chongum* (Sounds for the People) inscribed in 1446 shows the newly invented Korean alphabet (hangul) with explanations in classical Chinese. Hangul gave Koreans a means to write their own language in an easily learned form.

systems in the world. Its simple construction has made reading and writing easy for all Koreans. Chinese characters—once the only symbols used in written Korean—still appear in proper names and, along with the Korean alphabet, in a form of handwriting.

The Arts

Although Chinese influence on Korea was strong for centuries, artists and craftspeople on the Korean Peninsula developed distinctive forms of expression. Murals painted on the walls of tombs more than 1,500 years ago are among the earliest artworks found in Korea. Depictions of birds, animals, and human figures in the paintings found in Koguryo (present-day North Korea) are especially lively and colorful.

From about the fifth century until the rise of the Choson dynasty in 1392, Buddhism was the main artistic influence in Korea. Artists carved images of Buddha

Courtesy of Korean Overseas Information Services

Intricate, colorful patterns that incorporate good-luck symbols adorn traditional Korean wooden structures.

In 1985 Pak Saeng-kwang painted *Masks* to represent an ancient Korean folk art.

The Mountain and the Moon by Kim Whan-ki is a modern adaptation of a traditional theme in Korean art.

47

At the Korean Folk Village, which reenacts life during the Choson dynasty, a wood-carver turns out expressive masks that represent common characters—such as monks, housewives, and aristocrats—in masked dances.

—such as the one in Sokkuram, a cave temple near Kyongju—from bronze or stone. Stone pagodas (religious shrines) and temples were built, including the Pulguksa Temple near Kyongju.

One of the outstanding crafts of Korean artists has been ceramics. Celadon (bluish green porcelain) from the Koryo period (918 to 1392) displays intricate designs of birds, flowers, and other figures. Pottery from the Choson dynasty is simpler than celadon, and it strongly influenced Japanese art.

During the Choson dynasty, Confucianism replaced Buddhism as the primary influence on the arts in Korea. Scholars cultivated Chinese poetry, calligraphy (ornate handwriting), and landscape painting. In addition, a uniquely Korean style of painting developed during this period among less-educated Koreans. These folk paintings depicted the daily life of common

Sin Yun-bok painted the *Outdoor Party* in about 1800. Patterned after Chinese artistic styles, the work is characteristic of much of the Korean art produced during the Choson dynasty.

Calligraphy is a fine art that was practiced among the scholar-officials of the Choson dynasty.

people in Korean settings rather than in Chinese or idealized places. Some of these works reflected shamanism by portraying nature gods.

Literature

Much of Korean literature developed on two social levels. The upper classes composed poetry, and ordinary people cherished tales and songs. Among the wealthy, a short lyric poem known as the *sijo* arose in the twelfth century and occupies a distinctive place in Korean literature. Simple and expressive, these poems describe the beauty of nature, enjoyment of life, and philosophical thoughts. Scholars often composed sijo for special occasions, and South Koreans still write in this poetic form.

Individual expression, independence, and purity have long been important themes for Korean writers. The fleeting nature of time, the pleasures of family life, and loyalty to the state are other popular topics.

Among common people, myths and legends inspired *pansori,* which are long ballads chanted by a traveling minstrel to drum accompaniment. Three of the best-known pansori are *The Tale of Sim Chong,* about a devoted daughter who helps to restore her blind father's sight; *The Tale of Chun Hyang,* a love story; and *The Tale of Hungbu and Nolbu,* about a virtuous younger brother and his wicked older brother.

Contemporary Korean literature often expresses social and political ideas. After the Korean War, suffering, chaos, and moral confusion became common themes. The poems of Kim Chi-ha, such as "Five Bandits" and "The Story of a Sound," express anger toward government corruption and brutality.

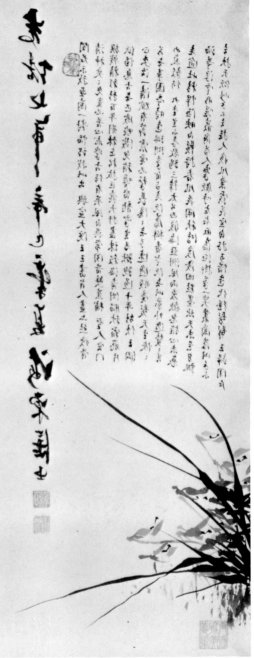

Courtesy of Korean Overseas Information Services

Music and Dance

Korean music has its roots in Confucian rituals, in court music, in Buddhist chants, and in folk music. Courtly music is slow, solemn, and complex. The dances of the

49

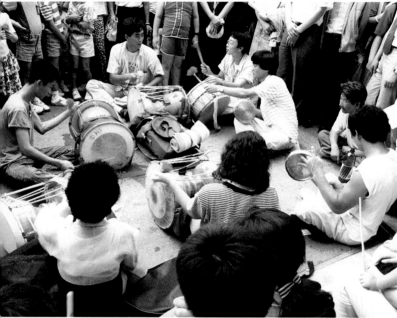

The *changgo* (hourglass drum) has two heads. Drummers strike the thick skin on the left side with their palms to produce a deep, muted tone. The thin skin on the right side, in contrast, creates a sharp, harsh sound and is struck with a stick. Because the changgo is used for many kinds of music, it is one of South Korea's most popular instruments.

Although Korea has not had a royal family since 1910, the court orchestra still plays on ritual occasions and for public performances. Two types of zithers are prevalent in Korean court music. The *komungo* has 6 strings stretched over 16 movable bridges and dates back to the seventh century. The *kayagum* has 12 strings and is very popular because of its versatility.

Courtesy of Korean Overseas Information Services

Dancers perform the *Hwagwanmu* (Flower Crown Dance) to the accompaniment of the court orchestra. The dancers wear a small crown, from which the dance takes its name, as well as long sleeves that flow over their hands. Performers swirl the sleeves to add color and excitement to their otherwise slow, graceful steps.

court are stately and formal. Ancient instruments include zithers (which have several strings stretched over a shallow, horizontal soundboard), flutes, reed instruments, and percussion. Drum alone usually accompanies the human voice to mark the beat.

Folk music, in contrast, is usually fast and lively, with vigorous, athletic dancing. Irregular rhythms are characteristic, and metal gongs, a *changgo* (a drum shaped like an hourglass), and a loud, trumpetlike oboe are common folk instruments.

Some modern Korean composers have drawn from themes in traditional music, but Western models have also influenced

A *mudang* (shamanist priestess) calls forth spirits in the *Salpuri,* or Exorcism Dance. Her movements bring her into a trance, cleansing her spirit of anguish and sweeping her audience from sadness to ecstatic joy. Traditionally, this dance is one of the rites performed in a *kut*—a shamanist ritual to release evil spirits from a sick person's body.

Courtesy of Korean Overseas Information Services

South Korea's contemporary music. The country has several symphony orchestras, opera companies, and music colleges, and South Korean performers have begun to gain international recognition.

Sports

South Koreans consider athletic activity very important, and they encourage children to pursue physical competition in sporting events. The activities range from modern to traditional games and include both individual and team sports. South Koreans are enthusiastic both as spectators and as participants.

Some of the most popular sports in South Korea are of Western origin. The British introduced soccer to Korea in 1882. Six professional and numerous amateur soccer teams compete each year. Baseball, volleyball, basketball, skiing, and table tennis arrived in the early twentieth century. More recent additions to South Korea's athletic activities include golf, archery, skating, and swimming.

Of South Korea's traditional physical activities, perhaps the best known are *ssirum* and *taekwondo*. Ssirum, an ancient form of wrestling, is at least 1,500 years old. Taekwondo is a self-defense martial art that has been evolving for 2,000 years. In modern times, the sport has gained popularity throughout the world, and South Korean instructors teach it in many countries.

South Korea hosts national and international sporting events in facilities built for the 1988 Olympics.

Taekwondo, or "the art of kicking and punching," combines abrupt and circular patterns along with jumping, blocking, and dodging techniques.

Courtesy of Korea National Tourism Corporation

Experts teach the age-old Korean form of wrestling known as *ssirum* as a formal course in South Korea's middle and high schools. Popular for centuries, the sport now appears on television during professional competitions.

Courtesy of Korea National Tourism Corporation

Individual athletic activities in South Korea include skiing, which is becoming increasingly popular.

Courtesy of Korea National Tourism Corporation

53

A busy port in South Korea reflects the nation's growing prominence in international trade.

4) The Economy

The division of the Korean Peninsula in 1945 and the subsequent Korean War seriously disrupted the Korean economy. Since the 1960s, however, South Korea has experienced dramatic economic growth. In 1945 the south had most of the agricultural resources but few industries or mineral resources. Many refugees entered South Korea from the north, which burdened the South Korean economy. The nation maintains a large and expensive army, which also drains its financial resources.

Despite these setbacks, by the late 1980s South Korea had developed its industrial and service sectors and had entered the international economic arena. In 1961 the average South Korean's share of the gross national product (GNP)—the total value of goods and services produced each year—was only $82. By 1986 that figure had risen to $2,370, which reflected a vastly improved standard of living for South Korea's people.

Various factors have contributed to South Korea's economic success. For example, Japan laid the groundwork for Korea's development during the colonial period. After the Korean War, the South Korean government took an active role in land reform and in industrial development. A skilled labor force that has been willing to work hard despite low wages has freed industrialists to focus on further development rather than on labor concerns.

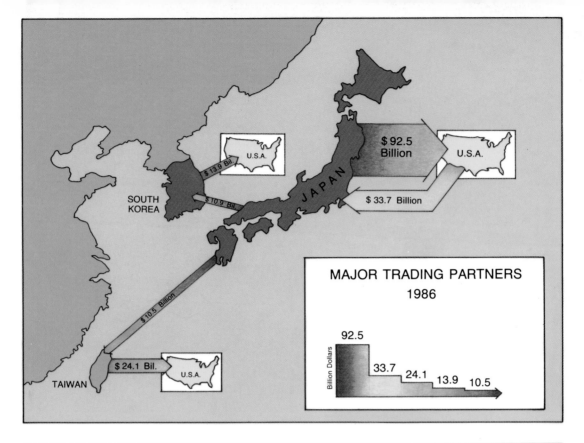

MAJOR TRADING PARTNERS
1986

Billion Dollars

92.5

33.7 24.1 13.9 10.5

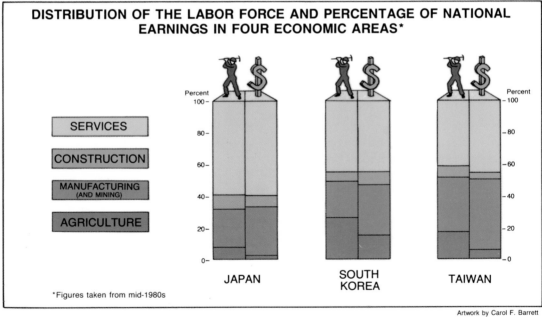

DISTRIBUTION OF THE LABOR FORCE AND PERCENTAGE OF NATIONAL EARNINGS IN FOUR ECONOMIC AREAS*

SERVICES

CONSTRUCTION

MANUFACTURING
(AND MINING)

AGRICULTURE

Percent
100 —

80 —

60 —

40 —

20 —

0 —

Percent
— 100

— 80

— 60

— 40

— 20

— 0

JAPAN

SOUTH
KOREA

TAIWAN

*Figures taken from mid-1980s

Artwork by Carol F. Barrett

The economies of Japan, South Korea, and Taiwan – the most industrialized nations in eastern Asia – depend on international trade. Outgoing and incoming arrows on the map show, respectively, the major export and import trading partners for each country. The width of the arrows illustrates the volume of the transactions in U.S. dollars. South Korea sells most of its exports to the United States and buys most of its imports from Japan. South Korea's trade surplus is suggested by a wider outgoing than incoming arrow. The graph in the lower right corner of the map compares the differences in dollar value between the arrow widths.

On the lower table, the left side of each bar reflects the percentage of the work force involved in four economic sectors. The bar's right side shows the percentage of the gross domestic product – the value of goods and services produced within the country – earned by each of the four areas. Agriculture once accounted for most of the economic activity in these countries. As each nation became more industrialized, however, its income depended less on farming and more on manufacturing and services (banking, trade, transportation, and health care, for example). (Data taken from *1988 Britannica Book of the Year.*)

As South Korea builds more automobile assembly plants, exports of cars and trucks increase.

Courtesy of Korean Overseas Information Services

Industry and Trade

South Korea has one of the world's fastest growing industrial economies. Industry accounts for about 35 percent of the GNP and employs 25 percent of the work force. Private owners control almost all of South Korea's industry.

In the 1950s, South Korea's factories focused on making labor-intensive light industrial items, such as textiles and processed food. Cotton, wool, and synthetic fabrics continue to be major exports. Food processing and the manufacture of clothing, shoes, and textiles employ more South Koreans than do any other industries.

Gradually, the nation has developed heavy industry and chemical processing plants, which together now account for over half of the total manufacturing out-

put. The nation is among the world's top producers of ships. The Pohang Iron and Steel Company has one of the world's largest and most efficient steel plants. At Changwon, a huge industrial complex produces various kinds of machinery. A growing electronics industry supplies foreign markets with radios, televisions, microwave ovens, and computers. Companies such as Lucky Goldstar, Daewoo, and Samsung—leading producers of household electronics—have earned South Korea a reputation for high-quality goods.

Production of automobiles has also increased, and cars have become the nation's third largest export, after textiles and electronics. Several large oil refineries process crude oil, which is then used in the production of plastics, synthetic rubber, and other petrochemical materials. Other products made in South Korea include chemical fertilizers, pesticides, paper, plywood, ceramics, and rubber tires.

South Korea's change from an agricultural to an industrial economy has spurred a boom in construction, which accounts for about one-fifth of the nation's industrial output. Factories, office and apartment buildings, highways, and water and sewer systems are expanding to meet the needs of a modern society. In addition, 5 percent of the industrial output comes from mining, which primarily consists of tungsten and anthracite (a high-grade coal).

Lacking many natural resources of its own, South Korea must import large amounts of raw materials—such as crude oil, iron, steel, and chemicals—for use in its factories. The nation exports a variety of finished products, including automobiles, clothing, electronic devices, fish, shoes, ships, and textiles. South Korean companies trade primarily with the United States, Japan, West Germany, and Saudi Arabia. South Korea's increasing industrial output has enabled the nation to develop a trade surplus—that is, the country now earns more money from its exports than it spends on imports.

Industrial growth has brought about a construction boom in South Korea. Known for their skill, speed, and low wages, teams of South Korean workers also operate abroad, especially in Third-World countries.

Courtesy of Korean Overseas Information Services

Courtesy of Korean Overseas Information Services
South Korea's iron and steel industry has grown quickly in recent years.

Agriculture

Once the mainstay of the South Korean economy, agriculture now accounts for only about 15 percent of the GNP and employs 25 percent of the work force. Almost all farms are privately owned, and landholdings average about 2.5 acres in size. Less than one-quarter of the nation's area is suitable for farming, and most of this land is mountainous. The terrain makes mechanized equipment difficult to use, and agricultural methods remain largely based on manual labor.

Over half of South Korea's farmland produces rice, the principal crop. On the western and southern coasts, a combination of heat and high humidity is ideal for growing rice. Farmers can plant two crops

Photo by David Gonnerman
Although only about one-quarter of South Korea's land is suitable for farming, that portion is rich and fertile.

Courtesy of Korea National Tourism Corporation

Some South Korean farmers raise silkworms—caterpillars that feed on mulberry leaves and then spin cocoons made of a highly prized fiber called silk. An important export as well as the basis of traditional Korean garments, silk can be dyed bright colors and is woven into cloth that is sold at markets such as this one in Seoul.

A South Korean woman gathers up red peppers that have been dried in the sun. Hot pepper is an essential spice in Korean cooking.

Photo by David Gonnerman

Rice — a labor-intensive crop that requires much hand work — is South Korea's principal agricultural item.

Independent Picture Service

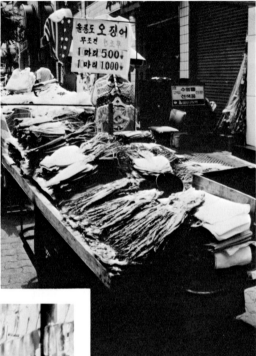

Photo by David Gonnerman

Courtesy of Korea National Tourism Corporation

Fishermen take in hauls of squid from the coastal waters surrounding South Korea. The catch is hung to dry *(left)* and is sold in both local *(above)* and foreign markets.

The hills of the South Korean countryside support forest reserves that are carefully monitored to protect the nation's timber industry.

a year in these regions, often alternating rice in the summer with barley in the winter. Since many South Koreans have immigrated to cities to find better employment, a shortage of workers has arisen on farms. Machines for transplanting and harvesting rice are beginning to answer the need for labor.

Other main food crops include sweet potatoes and yams. Some farmers grow corn, wheat, soybeans, cotton, white radishes, and Chinese cabbages. Orchards with apples, peaches, and pears are a new and important source of fruit. Cheju Island supports a large crop of oranges. Farmers are raising more livestock, because as South Koreans make more money they can afford to buy meat. Some farms raise silkworms, which produce the fiber from which silk fabric is made.

Forestry and Fishing

By 1970 loggers had harvested many of the trees that once covered two-thirds of South Korea. An active reforestation program, which began in the early 1970s, has more than doubled the volume of timber growing in the region. Forestry workers plant new trees each year, protect old ones, and develop new varieties that are more resistant to pests and disease. The government is strictly monitoring tree cutting until the forests are fully restocked. By limiting the amount of timber that is harvested, South Korea has also controlled the effects of flooding and erosion, which cause more damage on bare land.

With a modern fleet of more than 800 deep-sea vessels, South Korea is one of the world's leading fishing nations. The industry provides South Koreans not only with their main source of protein but also with a valuable export. Deep-sea fishing brings in part of the catch, which is then processed at the ports of Ulsan and Masan. The fleet fishes for tuna in waters as far away as Africa. In recent years, however, the size of the take has not increased. This lack of growth is due partly to the 200-mile fishing zones that many countries have claimed off their coasts.

Over 73,000 coastal fishing boats operate in the waters around South Korea.

A combination of private, public, and traditional means of transport fills a street in Seoul.

Pollack, squid, octopus, anchovies, crabs, and mackerel flourish in local waters. Aquaculture—which produces edible seaweed and oysters—is an important coastal fishing activity. Many farmers supplement their income by fishing.

Transportation

Although many South Koreans do not own cars, well-developed public transit provides service within and between cities. Trains and buses run frequently, and Seoul and Pusan have subway systems. In rural

A statue at Inchon commemorating the Korean War serves as a reminder of the bitter division of the Korean Peninsula.

areas, many people ride bicycles for short trips.

Construction teams are expanding the nation's expressways to decrease travel time and to encourage industrial development throughout the country. Of South Korea's 31,700 miles of roads, about half are paved. In addition, the state-owned railway system consists of 3,900 miles of track.

Airports located throughout the country also decrease domestic travel time. Korean Airlines, a privately owned company, flies to major cities within South Korea as well as to Japan, the United States, Taiwan, Hong Kong, Sri Lanka, Southeast Asia, the Middle East, and Europe.

The Future

South Korea—a nation that experienced rapid industrialization during the 1980s—faces many challenges. While its economy has grown dramatically, wages have not risen as fast. Workers have begun to organize and demonstrate for increased pay, for fewer hours, and for safer working conditions. Although democracy frequently follows economic progress, it remains to be seen whether South Korea's leaders will overcome their history of strict rule.

Some South Koreans say that democracy will be achieved only when the nation reunites with North Korea. This debate has sparked unrest among South Korean students since 1986. Some South Koreans believe that the presence of U.S. military bases in South Korea is slowing reunification efforts. Middle-class citizens, however, often view the government of Communist North Korea as a bigger threat to their country than the U.S. bases. Until South Koreans can agree on a way to gain more democratic reforms and on how to achieve reunification, the nation's continued success remains uncertain.

Photo by R. K. Hur

Many of South Korea's young people are politically aware and active. They seek both democracy and reunification of the Korean Peninsula—hopes shared by many of the nation's people.

63

Index